MW00878452

5 Most Powerful Promises and Prayers on Health and Healing

Get Quick Results Through Meditation and Prayer

(ENJOY FREE PROMISES BOOK 1)

FRANCIS JONAH

IMPORTANT

My name is Francis Jonah. I believe all things are possible. It is because of this belief that I have achieved so much in life. This belief extends to all. I believe every human being is equipped to succeed in every circumstance, regardless of the circumstance.

I know the only gap that exists between you and what you need to achieve or overcome is knowledge.

People are destroyed for lack of knowledge.

It is for this reason that I write short practical books that are so simple, people begin to experience immediate results as evidenced by the many testimonies I receive on a daily basis for my various books.

This book is no exception. You will obtain results because of it.

Visit my website for powerful articles and materials

www.francisjonah.com

FREE GIFT

Just to say Thank You for buying my book, I'd like to give you these books for free.

Get these 4 powerful books today for free and give yourself a great future.

Go to my website www.francisjonah.com to download for free

Your testimonies will abound. Check out my other books. They have produced many testimonies and I want your testimony to be one too.

Counselling Or Prayer

Send me an email if you need prayer or counsel or you have a question.

Better still if you want to make my acquaintance

My email is drfrancisjonah@gmail.com

Other books by Francis Jonah

1

Contents

INTRODUCTION

Note: The introduction and chapter one are essential foundations for all the books in the series.

As such these two have been repeated in all the books in the series to ensure that all who read them get the foundation.

When you understand that God is not a man to lie nor the son of man to change His mind, then you can be rest assured that His promises will not fail.

The best part of His promises is that in Christ, they are no more promises, they are realities.

In Christ, God's promise to you is 'Yes' and only 'Yes'.

For all the promises of God in him *are* yea, and in him Amen, unto the glory of God by us.

2 Corinthians 1:20

By these promises therefore, we are confident of dominating every circumstance that we will come up against. By these promises, we are sure to operate on the level of divinity.

The realm of divinity gives us the edge over the natural and human realm. To know that it is the promises of God that usher us into that realm is amazing. It means we can use the promises of God to operate in our divine nature:

Whereby are given unto us exceeding great and precious promises: that by these ye might be partakers of the divine nature, having escaped the corruption that is in the world through lust.

2 Peter 1:4

Think of it this way, for your success in life and every circumstance that you would ever face, God says **"what will see you through are my promises"**. Not only that, He guarantees these promises in Christ Jesus.

It means every promise of God is **guaranteed** - guaranteed to work in the life of every believer.

Christ is our guarantee. Glory to God. If He is our guarantee, God's promises for us will never fail.

In this book are 5 powerful promises and prayers that will make health and healing a perpetual part of your life.

The book is concise and straight to the point; the value it will deliver to you is amazing.

Get ready to see real progress in your life.

In my own life, I have never been so sure of the goodness of God and I daily bask in the realities of His promises for me.

This book will awaken something within you. You do not need to know 500 promises to succeed in life. A few important and powerful promises, if understood, meditated upon and applied correctly will cause tremendous results in the life of every individual believer.

You will be a partaker of the divine nature. You will see the blessings of God at work in your life. You will know how to pray the promises of God and have a working mind-set that will lead from victory to victory.

There are also prayers backing every promise for your benefit.

You will meditate and you will pray and you will produce results. In Jesus name. Amen.

CHAPTER ONE:

PROMISES

A promise is a commitment to do or not to do something.

It could also be a commitment to give or not to give something.

Promises are necessary because uncertainty in any circumstance is a faith killer.

Promises are important so that any man or woman with a promise will know what to expect in any given situation.

In the case of God's promises, it is to give us a sense of assurance that He will be faithful to His words.

Thus we can know what to expect of Him in any given situation.

God's promises are not flippant or casual; they are rock-solid commitments by God himself. He is stuck to them like glue.

That is why we must take His promises seriously. It is because He takes them seriously.

HIS WORD IS HIS PROMISE

If you have ever wondered what the promise of God is, then you must understand that His word is His promise.

We make promises with words. In that same way, God has made promises to us through His words.

By taking a look at the word of God, you will see so many things God has said in His word that He will do or will not do.

These are the basis of joy for every believer because with such a foundation, anyone can build his or her life. Foundations like this are a great start to build your life:

for he hath said, I will never leave thee, nor forsake thee. Hebrews 13:5b

That is what God has said. It is His promise. You can rest in it. He will never leave you. He will never forsake you. I am feeling confident already. No matter what, God never leaves me nor forsakes me. He never leaves me despite what men and pastors say.

HIS WORD STANDS SUPREME

God's words stand supreme above all else. They stand so supreme, He has actually exalted them above all His names.

That should tell every believer the integrity attached to every promise of God. God will not break his word. He has willingly submitted and tied

Himself to His word.

For whose sake will God go to the extent of exalting His word above His name?

It is for the sake of the believer, so that we can know beyond every reasonable doubt that we can trust in His promises.

It simply means God has made His word more important than His name. Father, thank You so much for such care.

Such blessedness. We know we can trust His promises because He has exalted His them above His name. He is subject to His own words. He has bound Himself to them. Scripture puts it beautifully:

I will worship toward thy holy temple, and praise thy name for thy loving kindness and for thy truth: <u>for thou hast magnified thy word above all thy name</u>. Psalm 138:2

GOD IS SO SERIOUS ABOUT HIS PROMISES

God is so serious about His promises, He swears by Himself just to show how serious He is.

I don't know which other god can go to this extent to prove his seriousness. But our Father God does, so that we also can attach a level of seriousness to the promises He has given to us.

In promising Abraham, He said:

And said, By myself have I sworn, saith the LORD, for because thou hast done this thing, and hast not withheld thy son, thine only *son:*
That in blessing I will bless thee, and in multiplying I will multiply thy seed as the stars of the heaven, and as the sand which *is* **upon the sea shore; and thy seed shall possess the gate of his enemies;**
Genesis 22:16-17

SWEARING BY HIMSELF

God swore by Himself in this way:

And said, By myself have I sworn, saith the LORD, for because thou hast done this thing, and hast not withheld thy son, thine only *son:*

That in blessing I will bless thee, and in multiplying I will multiply thy seed as the stars of the heaven, and as the sand which *is* **upon the sea shore; and thy seed shall possess the gate of his enemies;**

Genesis 22:16-17

God swore by Himself because there was no one greater to swear by. He was holding Himself accountable should there be any slackness in performing the promise.

He did all this to give Abraham assurance. Assurance or certainty is key in the Christian faith. A double-minded man is very unstable in all his ways and will not receive anything from God.

That is how serious uncertainty is. It causes you not to receive anything from God although God has given you everything you will ever need in life.

That act by God was to settle any doubt in the mind of Abraham.

In the same way, God wants you to remove every doubt in your mind regarding His promises. He is faithful to them. All He needs is your seriousness about his promises.

He wants you to receive them and has done everything to remove doubt and double mindedness.

HIS WORD DOES NOT RETURN VOID

God is so good that, His words do not return unto Him void. They perform that to which they are sent.

The word of God is not designed to return to Him void. It is designed to perform what it was sent to perform, nothing else. There is no retreat, no surrender with God's word. Always forward moving.

The Bible puts it beautifully. It says:

So shall my word be that goeth forth out of my mouth: it shall not return unto me void, but it shall accomplish that which I please, and it shall prosper in the thing whereto I sent it.

Isaiah 55:11

If the word of God does not return unto Him void, you should know the power of His word.

God is so concerned about His word coming to pass in your life that He has designed it not to come unto Him void.

It means His promises are not supposed to come to heaven, they are supposed to work on earth.

The reason is that, it is His desire that His promises come to pass in your life.

We serve a good God.

We serve a living God.

GOD IS NOT A MAN

Men lie. Men promise and fail. Men are specialists in disappointment. If you use your experience with men to relate to God, your trust will not be complete.

God is not a man.

He doesn't lie. He doesn't disappoint. He doesn't fail.

With such attributes, you can put your trust in Him.

If you know God very well, you will not have trust issues with Him. If you have issues trusting Him, then you need to get to the basics and know Him very well. You know Him by studying the Bible.

See what the Bible says:

God is not a man, that he should lie; neither the son of man, that he should repent: hath he said,

and shall he not do it? Or hath he spoken, and shall he not make it good?

Numbers 23:19

When you know Him, you will know who you are dealing with and if you know who you are dealing with, you will trust Him completely.

When God says, He does. It is that simple, you can take Him at His word.

IMPORTANT: DO YOUR PART

Understand this, when you do your part, you will receive what God promised.

The reason is simple. God has already moved, we just have to respond to see His hand in our lives.

He is not about to move. He has already moved. He declares the end from the beginning.

We must respond to what He has made available and it will manifest in our lives.

See here:

Isa 46:10 Declaring the end from the beginning, and from ancient times the things that are not yet done, saying, My counsel shall stand, and I will do all my pleasure:

God declares the end from the beginning. He has already moved ahead of us.

We are not waiting for Him to move. He is waiting for us to move.

We are not waiting for Him to bless us, He is waiting of us to receive and respond to His blessing.

He said He has already blessed us with all spiritual blessings in Heavenly places in Christ Jesus. Please read carefully and understand that it is past tense. It is already done.

Eph 1:3 Blessed be the God and Father of our Lord Jesus Christ, who hath blessed us with all spiritual blessings in heavenly places in Christ:

Ephesians 1:3

We are not waiting for Him to heal us, He already carried our infirmities, He is waiting for us to receive the healing:

Mat 8:17 That it might be fulfilled which was spoken by Esaias the prophet, saying, Himself took our infirmities, and bare our sicknesses.

He is waiting for us to receive and respond to the healing He has provided.

Glory. He already carried our sicknesses and took our infirmities. Meditate on the realities of this revelation.

This is the reason we must be aggressive about our approach. The reason is simple. The promises and provisions are already provided and available.

We are the ones not aggressive in receiving and responding to it.

We are not waiting for Him to increase us, He is waiting for us to receive increase.

Change your mind-set today and possess your possessions.

Oba 1:17 But upon mount Zion shall be deliverance, and there shall be holiness; and the house of Jacob shall possess their possessions.

Obadiah 1:17

Possessing your possessions is an active business. Do not be passive about it.

Let us move into the promises and prayers that will give you assurance of health and healing.

CHAPTER TWO

FIRST PROMISE AND PRAYER

Please note that the promises must be meditated upon day and night till results show. Same with the prayers.

The first promise on health and healing we will look at is in the book of 1st Peter:

1 Pe 2:24 Who his own self bare our sins in his own body on the tree, that we, being dead to sins, should live unto righteousness: by whose stripes ye were healed.

1 Peter 2:24

The first promise you need to meditate on for health and healing makes it clear that healing has already been provided for you.

Jesus bore our sins in His body and also took stripes on his body.

The two things Jesus did above brought about two results:

1. Our sins were forgiven

2. Our diseases were healed.

By the two acts of bearing sins in His body and receiving stripes, Jesus made available the forgiveness of sins and the healing of our bodies.

Just like your sins have been paid for and you believe and agree to that truth, your healing has also been paid for.

Repeat it to yourself:

My healing has been paid for.

If your healing has already been paid for, then receive your healing.

Lay hold on it and curse very sickness or evil spirit that wants to deprive you of that which has already been paid for on your behalf.

By his stipes you were healed.

God had made provision for your healing before you ever got sick.

That is why He is a good God.

He wants you well, that is why He made provision for your health and healing.

Meditate on the scripture till it is planted firmly in your heart and confess that:

My healing has been paid for.

It is interesting to know that Peter was making reference to Isaiah when he said this:

Isa 53:5 But he was wounded for our transgressions, he was bruised for our iniquities: the chastisement of our peace was upon him; and with his stripes we are healed.

Isaiah 53:5

Your healing was established long ago in prophecy. Jesus only came to fulfil the condition for your healing.

Once the condition was fulfilled the prophecy became activated.

Payment for your healing was already spoken about. Provision has now been made for your healing. Take it with everything you have.

While you take it, take it by force. It belongs to you and the devil will not rob you of it.

Have this mind-set when dealing with sickness. Sicknesses and diseases are thieves, trying to rob you of what has already been paid for and given to you.

Resist them. They are not your portion.

Don't suffer for something you are not supposed to suffer for.

Prayer

Father, in the name of Jesus, I come before You and thank You for making provision for my healing and health.

Thank You for the stripes of Jesus that was payment for my healing.

Now, in Jesus name, I receive my healing.

Devil, you are a liar. I command you, out of my body.

In Jesus name. Go with all your associated pain and symptoms. Now.

You thief, out of my life.

Thank You Father, because it is done.

Take the praise. Take the adoration. In Jesus name. Amen.

CHAPTER THREE

SECOND PROMISE AND PRAYER

The second promise and prayer on health and healing we will look at is in the book of Psalms:

Psa 103:2 Bless the LORD, O my soul, and forget not all his benefits:

Psa 103:3 Who forgiveth all thine iniquities; who healeth all thy diseases;

Psalm 103:2-3

The second promise you need to meditate on makes it clear that God does two things for us. According to the above verses of scripture:

1. He forgives all our iniquities

2. He heals all our diseases

I want you to take note of the absolute terms used.

God doesn't forgive some of your sins as a believer and leave some. He forgives all of them.

Secondly God does not heal some of your sicknesses and claim that some cannot be healed.

He heals all your diseases.

It doesn't matter what the disease is and how long it has been with you.

It doesn't also matter what you did or did not do to cause that disease.

Whether it is cancer or any other terminal disease, God heals all.

Even if it is a simple headache too, God heals it too.

There is no disease too small or too big for God.

Settle it in your mind. God heals all your diseases.

He heals all your diseases.

Give God praise that there is no disease he cannot heal.

Glory to God.

Meditate on the statements below:

God heals all my diseases including the current disease afflicting me.

There is no disease too big or too small for my God. He heals all of them.

There is no sin or mistake God cannot forgive, He forgives all my sins and mistakes.

Prayer

Father, in the name of Jesus, I thank You that all my sins are forgiven.

I thank You that You heal **ALL** my diseases.

I decree that this disease of (...name of disease...) is healed in the name of Jesus.

It is not bigger than God or His promise of healing.

In the name of Jesus you infirmity called (....put name of disease...) go and never come back in Jesus name.

You will not rob me of what God has given to me.

Father, I thank you that you have healed this disease also. I give you all glory and praise.

In Jesus name. Amen.

CHAPTER FOUR

THIRD PROMISE AND PRAYER

The third promise and prayer on health and healing we will look at is in the book of James:

Jas 5:13 Is any among you afflicted? let him pray. Is any merry? let him sing psalms.

Jas 5:14 Is any sick among you? let him call for the elders of the church; and let them pray over him, anointing him with oil in the name of the Lord:

Jas 5:15 And the prayer of faith shall save the sick, and the Lord shall raise him up; and if he have committed sins, they shall be forgiven him.

James 5:13-15

The third promise we need to meditate on for health and healing makes it clear that the prayer of faith will heal anyone who is prayed for by the elders of the church.

There are people who die and suffer sickness when they shouldn't.

A simple invitation to the elders of the church or the pastors or anyone who is on fire for God can help fulfil the promise of being anointed with oil and the prayer of faith.

I have prayed for many people and they have received their healing.

I know one gentleman who applied oil I have prayed on over his boil.

The boil just disappeared.

Prayer by third parties especially those who have faith in God's word and being anointed by them will deliver healing quickly.

Understand this. The word of God has made provision that when a third party anoints you and prays the prayer of faith over you, your healing will be sure.

The Bible says the prayer of faith shall save the sick and God will raise him up.

If the person has committed sins, God shall forgive him.

All we need is to believe that when we invite the elders or those in good standing with God, all they need to do is to anoint and pray a prayer of faith.

That is all God needs to raise you up from your sick bed or condition.

God has made provision for my healing through the elders of the church. I receive that provision also. In Jesus name.

Prayer

Father, in the name of Jesus, I thank you for your provision of healing through the elders of the church or any third party who is right with you.

I pray direct me to whom I should invite.

I also pray and release angels to bring such people my way. In Jesus name.

Amen.

CHAPTER FIVE

FOURTH PROMISE AND PRAYER

The fourth promise and prayer on health and healing we will look at is in the book of Matthew:

Mat 8:17 That it might be fulfilled which was spoken by Esaias the prophet, saying, Himself took our infirmities, and bare our sicknesses.

Matthew 8:17

The fourth promise you need to meditate on for health and healing makes it clear that Jesus Christ carried your infirmities and bare your sicknesses.

This simply means that Jesus Christ already carried and took upon himself the sicknesses and the infirmities you are also carrying now.

This is not done anywhere. Once someone is carrying your sickness, there is no need to carry it too.

If I am carrying your shoe, it means you shouldn't be carrying your shoe too.

If you are carrying your shoe, it is because someone has tricked you into believing that your shoe has not been carried.

The devil is just taking advantage of you by putting on you sicknesses and diseases Jesus already carried.

He is preying on your ignorance and stealing your health and killing you.

Today we know better. You will not allow the thief and liar to take advantage of you anymore.

You will not carry a sickness or disease someone else has carried for you.

It will be a grave error.

This revelation made me angry some time ago. I meditated on it so much that it became a part of me and the sicknesses I suffered run away.

They had to. I now knew the truth and I applied it aggressively.

That is how to treat the devil.

Be aggressive about resisting him and he will flee from you.

Let him know that you know he is a trickster who is tricking you into carrying a disease some else has carried for you.

It doesn't matter the disease. Whether it is diabetes, cancer, insomnia, stroke, infertility or what have you, all you need to know is that Jesus has already carried it.

Say this to yourself till it gets into your spirit man:

Jesus has carried my sicknesses, therefore, I do not need to carry them anymore.

From today, I let go of every sickness and disease I have carried and pampered. Jesus already carried it.

Prayer

Father, in the name of Jesus, I thank You that Jesus has already carried the (...name the disease...) I am also carrying.

Thank You for Your word of truth that has set me free.

I loose myself of that burden and bondage.

Sickness, from today, I do not carry you again. Depart from my body and never come back in Jesus name.

Devil, you are a liar and you have been exposed. Leave with your baggage and disgrace. Now.

Father, I thank You that the burden is lifted. Be glorified, I worship you, I praise You. Take all the magnification.

You deserve it because You are loving, kind and providing.

I pray in Jesus name. Amen

CHAPTER SIX

FIFTH PROMISE AND PRAYER

The fifth promise and prayer on health and healing we will look at is in the book of Deuteronomy:

Deu 7:14 Thou shalt be blessed above all people: there shall not be male or female barren among you, or among your cattle.

Deu 7:15 And the LORD will take away from thee all sickness, and will put none of the evil diseases of Egypt, which thou knowest, upon thee; but will lay them upon all them that hate thee.

Deuteronomy 7:14-15

The fifth promise you need to meditate on for health and healing makes it clear that God will take away from you all sickness.

When I tell people I have not been sick for 10 years, they find it difficult to believe.

But God is always true and His word has stood the test of time.

Admittedly, when I began to meditate on this scripture plus one in Isaiah that says no one living in Zion will say I am sick, I occasionally fell sick.

But I believed the word despite my circumstances.

How I stopped falling sick, I cannot tell. All I know is that some way, somehow, I am now walking in the dimension of the promise of God. Where sickness has been taken away from me.

He has promised to take away all sicknesses from you.

No matter the sickness. Whether curable or incurable, He says He will take it away from you.

God says He will take sickness away from you. Are you ready to release the sickness you are holding on to?

God says He will take it away. Allow Him.

Once you allow Him, you will be free.

Meditate till these words enter into your spirit:

God says He will take all sickness away from me.

Today, I give him permission to take away every sickness I am holding on to.

Notice also that he says ALL sickness. It doesn't matter the sickness or how long it has afflicted you.

Know that God is willing to take it away if you will allow Him.

Prayer

Father, in the name of Jesus, You said You will take away all sickness from me.

Today I give you permission to take away this sickness of (...Name of sickness...).

I walk in the promise of not experiencing any sickness again.

Thank You for fulfilling Your promise in my life.

You spirit of infirmity, pack bag and baggage and leave my body now for you have been taken away from me in Jesus name.

I bless You Father and celebrate the victory.

Take all the glory and the praise in Jesus name.

CHAPTER SEVEN

IMPORTANT KEYS

There are certain important keys that I must leave with you to ensure maximum results.

These keys will be repeated in all the books in this series so that all can benefit from it.

Key number 1: Thanksgiving

Continually give God thanks for fulfilling his promise in your life.

People look at their problems, instead of looking at God and His promise.

If you look at the sickness, you won't thank God. That is why you must look at God and His promise. That way you can give great praise and see results.

Key number 2: Fasting and Prayer

What will be the use of the food you are eating if the sickness you are carrying kills you?

When things are tough, you need to enter into long fasts to remove unbelief and build faith so that you can deal with sickness once and for all.

I know people who give all sorts of excuses why they cannot fast.

Please exclude yourself from that category of people and do the needful.

Long fasts (14 to 40 days of water only) on their own without prayer have been known to deal with a lot of diseases including tumours and cancers.

Much more adding prayer to the fasts.

Read the account below and you will see the great power fasting releases in the life of a believer. It makes you accomplish the difficult or impossible.

Mat 17:14 And when they were come to the multitude, there came to him a certain man, kneeling down to him, and saying,

Mat 17:15 Lord, have mercy on my son: for he is lunatick, and sore vexed: for ofttimes he falleth into the fire, and oft into the water.

Mat 17:16 And I brought him to thy disciples, and they could not cure him.

Mat 17:17 Then Jesus answered and said, O faithless and perverse generation, how long shall I be with you? how long shall I suffer you? bring him hither to me.

Mat 17:18 And Jesus rebuked the devil; and he departed out of him: and the child was cured from that very hour.

Mat 17:19 Then came the disciples to Jesus apart, and said, Why could not we cast him out?

Mat 17:20 And Jesus said unto them, Because of your unbelief: for verily I say unto you, If ye have faith as a grain of mustard seed, ye shall say unto this mountain, Remove hence to yonder place; and it shall remove; and nothing shall be impossible unto you.

Mat 17:21 Howbeit this kind goeth not out but by prayer and fasting.

Matthew 17: 14 -21

If you are serious about your health and living long, fasting will be a decision you will easily make as a believer.

Key number 3: Sacrificial seed

You can sow a sacrificial seed to enter into a covenant with God for your absolute healing.

The practise was taught by David and practised by many in the Bible.

Psa 50:5 Gather my saints together unto me; those that have made a covenant with me by sacrifice.

Psalms 50:5

Sow your sacrificial seeds and see this personal covenant work on your behalf.

If you want to sow your sacrificial seed into a ministry that has blessed you and is blessing multitudes, you can sow it into my ministry.

I pray right now that your sacrifice will bring immediate results in Jesus name.

I pray healing and creative miracles over your life.

I release angels to bring your answer right now.

Whoever must have a change of heart for you to be blessed, I command that change of heart now. In Jesus name.

Click Here to sow your sacrificial seed and expect great results.

KEYS TO ESTABLISH EVERY PROMISE IN YOUR LIFE

1. "If you abide in Me, and My words abide in you, you will ask what you desire, and it shall be done for you." (John 15:7)

Once we believe in Jesus and meditate in His word, we have set ourselves up for continuous victory.

2. "If you have faith and do not doubt, you will not only do what was done to the fig tree, but also if you say to this mountain, 'Be removed and be cast into the sea,' it will be done." (Matthew 21:21)

We must build our faith by hearing the word and prayer. We must deal with doubt through fasting. That way, we can walk in powerful dimensions.

3. "If you can believe, all things are possible to him who believes." (Mark 9:23)

We can walk in dimensions unknown to men if only we can trust that all things are possible if we can believe.

4. "If you want to enter into life, keep the commandments." (Matthew 19:17)

Obedience has rewards hat sacrifice will never give to you. Pride and disobedience have cut off many people from god things that are available to them.

5. "If we ask anything according to His will, He hears us. And if we know that He hears us, whatever we ask, we know that we have the petitions that we have asked of Him." (1 John 5:14-15)

Praying the will of God guarantees answers. Let us study the word of God to know His will. It will

make our prayer lives simple and results will flow effortlessly.

You are blessed as you walk in the divine health and are healed of every disease.

REVIEW

Because your review is important to help others benefit from these books, please leave a good review.

This book is a part of a series of books on the promises of God.

The other books in the series are:

1. <u>5 Most Powerful promises and Prayers on Health and Healing</u>
2. <u>5 Most Powerful promises and Prayers on Finances</u>

Made in the USA
Middletown, DE
01 March 2021

34602239R00038